101 (at least!) ∧REASONS TO
GET UP IN THE MORNING
CELEBRITIES' FAVOURITE INSPIRATIONAL QUOTES

Julie Tanner

And Richard Briers

CANTERBURY
PRESS
Norwich

First published in 2005 by the Canterbury Press Norwich
(a publishing imprint of Hymns Ancient & Modern Limited,
a registered charity)
St Mary's Works, St Mary's Plain,
Norwich, Norfolk, NR3 3BH

www.scm-canterburypress.co.uk

British Library Cataloguing in Publication data

A catalogue record for this book is available
from the British Library

ISBN 1-85311-673-4/9781-85311-673-5

Typeset by Regent Typesetting, London
Printed and bound in Great Britain by
William Clowes Ltd, Beccles, Suffolk

Contents

This book is in memory of my friend, Andy Gard.

Author's Note

I like quotes because they can be as serious or as humorous as you want. They can be thought-provoking or mind-boggling.

This is my favourite inspirational quote:

To the world you may be one person, but to one person you may be the world.

This book consists of inspirational quotes by people who have achieved great things. I hope you enjoy reading it as much as I enjoyed researching it and putting it together.

I would like to thank all my friends and family for their support. Thanks also go to Alison Cox, Founder and Chief Executive of CRY who gave me the opportunity to do this. Special thanks go to my mum, who encouraged me throughout.

Julie Tanner (aged 12)

This book is part of CRY's 2005 10th Anniversary

CRY (Cardiac Risk in the Young)

Raising awareness of cardiac risk in the young, offering counselling and raising funds for cardiac screening and research (charity no. 1050845).

Julie Walters OBE

One of Britain's most accomplished actresses, whose films include Educating Rita, Billy Elliot, Harry Potter *(as Mrs Weasley) and* Calendar Girls.

Julie Walters

'Savour the day.'

The Most Revd and Rt Hon Dr Rowan Williams

The Archbishop of Canterbury since 2002.

'For I am sure that neither death, nor life, nor angels, nor principalities, nor things present, nor things to come, nor powers, nor height, nor depth, nor anything else in all creation, will be able to separate us from the love of God in Christ Jesus our Lord.'

Romans 8.38–39

Hugh Grant

*The well-known actor in theatre and TV,
and star of many films.*

'Work is more fun than fun.'

Noel Coward

Matt Holland

The Ireland international footballer and former Ipswich Town captain and player for Charlton Athletic FC.

'The only place success comes before work is in a dictionary!'

The Rt Hon Tony Blair

The British Prime Minister, elected in 1997 (Labour).

'Aim for the stars. If you aim for the stars you might have a chance of hitting the ceiling. If you aim for the ceiling you might fall flat on your face.'

Sir Matt Busby

John Inverdale

The sports presenter whose biggest sporting passion is rugby union.

'A Quote from Roger Federer at a press conference when he was asked if, at 2 sets down and 4–1 to Raphael Nadal, he thought he was going to be beaten.
He said simply: "The moment you think of defeat, you are lost."
Which is a good motto in the context, I thought.'

John's friend, Howard English, aged 32, died in his arms during a rugby match. Ten years later, Howard's son Seb aged 15, also died in a rugby match. Howard's genetic heart condition had not been diagnosed correctly in the post-mortem and so Seb was never tested.

George Cole OBE

The actor on stage, screen, radio and television, including playing the ever-optimistic spiv in the St Trinians' films and the secondhand car salesman Arthur Daley in the television series Minder.

'Yet meet we shall, and part, and meet again, where dead men meet, on the lips of living men.'

Samuel Butler

7

Joanna Trollope OBE

The best-selling author.

Joanna Trollope

'Death is not the extinguishing of the light, but the putting out of the lamp, because the dawn has come.'

Rabindranath Tagore

Sir Cliff Richard OBE

The singer and actor of over 40 years.

'To whom much is given, much is required – for greater is their responsibility.'

The New Testament

Sir Donald Sinden CBE

*The English actor who, with his distinctive voice, has
appeared on stage, television and radio, from classical
Shakespearean roles to comedy. He is a keen theatre historian
and one of the founders of the British Theatre Museum.*

'The lamentable change is from the best:
the worst returns to laughter.'

Shakespeare's King Lear

Sandi Toksvig

The writer and comedian whose television shows include Call My Bluff *and* Whose Line Is It Anyway? *and on radio* I'm Sorry I Haven't a Clue.

Sand Toksvig

'If no one ever took risks Michelangelo would have painted the Sistine floor.'

Neil Simon (US playwright)

Julia Sawalha

The actress who became well known in the role of Saffy in
Absolutely Fabulous.

'There is nothing enlightened about
shrinking so that other people will not
feel insecure around you.'

Nelson Mandela

Sir Terry Wogan OBE

The interviewer and presenter of documentary features, host of television quiz and variety shows and a writer and BBC radio presenter.

'The only difference between the "difficult" and the "impossible" is that the latter takes a little longer.'

Thomas Edison

Bob the Builder

The favourite children's animated character.

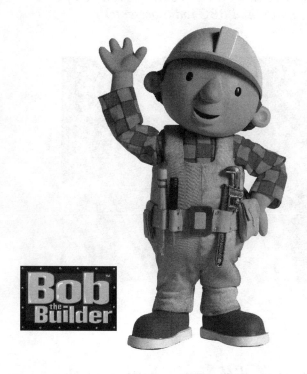

'Can we fix it? Yes we can!'

Jayne Torvill OBE

The former Olympic and World Champion ice-skater.

'God, grant me the serenity to accept the things I cannot change, courage to change the things I can, and wisdom to know the difference.'

Reinhold Niebuhr

Lord Brian Rix Kt CBE DL

The former British comedy actor and theatre manager, a campaigner for people with learning disabilities, and the President of Mencap.

'Dum vires annique sinunt, tolerate labores. Jam veniet tacito curva senecta pede.'

Ovid

LORD RIX Kt, CBE, DL

'While years and strength allow, tolerate work. Soon will come bent old age with silent foot.'

Gary Lineker OBE

England's leading World Cup goal-scorer.
Since 'retirement' he has become a regular BBC
football presenter.

'When Fate
hands you a
lemon, try to
make
lemonade.'

Dale Carnegie

Zoë Wanamaker CBE

The actress who has spent 25 years at the Royal Shakespeare Company and the National Theatre, and well known on TV in Love Hurts *and* My Family. *She has played in over 100 roles and performances, starring in the Harry Potter film as Madam Hooch. She is Trustee of The Globe Theatre.*

'May the force be with you.'

Ben Kenobi in *Star Wars*, George Lucas

Alan Titchmarsh MBE

The best-known gardener in the UK, he is a writer and the television presenter of Gardeners' World, Ground Force, *and the series* British Isles: A Natural History.

'Never let it be said that your mother bred a gibber.'

My grandad

Ann Widdecombe MP

The Conservative Member of Parliament for Maidstone and The Weald, and novelist.

Ann Widdecombe

'Carpe diem.' 'Seize the Day.'

Horace

Emma Thompson

The accomplished English actress of theatre, television and film who has won many awards.

'Only be original and never forget
HOW TO FAIL!'

My father

David Hemery CBE

*The 400m Olympic hurdler who broke the world record in
1968. In 1998 he was the first President of UK Athletics.*

'If you think you're too small to make a
difference, you've obviously never been
in bed with a mosquito!'

Anita Roddick

Chris Tarrant

The radio and television presenter, producer and writer.

Chris Tarrant

'Life's not a rehearsal – don't forget to smell the flowers.'

Nigel Planer

The actor and writer, performing in The Young Ones *as the hippy, Neil; a writer for* Not the Nine O'Clock News.

'Life is what happens while you're making other plans.'

John Lennon

The Rt Hon Jack Straw MP

The Secretary of State for Foreign and Commonwealth Affairs (Labour) and Member of Parliament for Blackburn.

'Ah, but a man's reach should exceed his grasp, Or what's a heaven for?'

Robert Browning

Sally Gunnell OBE

The former athlete and hurdler, and the only woman to hold four titles at the same time: Olympic, World, European and Commonwealth. She is also a television presenter.

**'Enthusiasm in your feelings.
Clarity in your thoughts.
Strength in your will.'**

Sir Robin Knox-Johnston CBE

*The first person to sail single-handed non-stop
around the world.*

'Oh Lord, if
we are marked
to die, I had
rather it were
in proceeding
than in
retreating.'

John Cavendish, a great navigator in the reign of
Elizabeth I, who was battering his way westward
through the Magellan Straits with most of his crew
sick

Ken Livingstone

The Mayor of London since 2000.

'We will leave this City, not less, but greater and more beautiful than it was left to us.'

From the Athenian Oath

Dame Tanni Grey Thompson

The greatest British paralympic athlete, with 11 gold medals, and a much-loved and respected TV and radio presenter.

This is something that my grandfather used to say and I have used it as inspiration throughout my sporting career:

'Aim high even if you hit a cabbage.'

Delia Smith OBE

The cookery writer and broadcaster.

'God's Grandeur

The world is charged with the grandeur of God.
  It will flame out, like shining from shook foil;
  It gathers to a greatness, like the ooze of oil
Crushed. Why do men then now not reck his rod?
Generations have trod, have trod, have trod;

And all is seared with trade; bleared, smeared
   with toil;
And wears man's smudge and shares man's
   smell: the soil
Is bare now, nor can foot feel, being shod.

And, for all this, nature is never spent;
   There lives the dearest freshness deep down
     things;
And though the last lights off the black West went
   Oh, morning, at the brown brink eastwards,
     springs –
Because the Holy Ghost over the bent
   World broods with warm breast and what ah!
     bright wings.'

Gerard Manley Hopkins

The Rt Hon
Charles Kennedy MP

The leader of the Liberal Democrat Party and Member of Parliament for Ross, Skye and Inverness West since 1997.

'We can only make the most of the future if we are clear about what we want to achieve.'

'It is vital to uphold the principles of honesty and integrity, not only to restore a sense of faith and trust in the political process, but also in everyday life.'

Robert Jones MBE

The Welsh professional rugby player, National Training and Development Manager, and CRY Patron.

'Success is the peace of mind of knowing that you've given your very best to become the very best you can be.'

John Wooden, former basketball coach

Robert had been fundraising for CRY in memory of a friend's young son who had been found dead, when his own family suffered the same devastating tragedy with the sudden cardiac death of the cousin he had grown up with.

Pete Goss MBE

The yachtsman who became the fastest British sailor to sail single-handed around the world in 126 days and 21 hours. He was awarded the MBE and France's highest decoration, the Legion d'Honneur, after his heroic rescue of Raphael Dinelli during the single-handed Round the World Race in 1996. He is also a public speaker.

'Life hangs on a very thin thread and the cancer of time is complacency. If you want to do something then do it NOW. Tomorrow is too late.'

Sir John Mills CBE

The actor, producer and director: a distinguished star whose career spanned 8 decades. After 60 years of marriage he and his wife Mary renewed their marriage vows having been denied a church service because he was serving in the Army during World War II. He died in 2005.

'To thine own self be true.'

Polonius, in Shakespeare's *Hamlet*

Graham Gooch OBE

The England and Essex cricketer and former Captain, and the Head Coach of Essex Cricket Club.

'Many have the will to win, but few have the will to prepare.'

Nicholas Lyndhurst

The actor who became famous as Rodney in
Only Fools and Horses.

'Wherever you go – there you are!'

Zen saying

Jeremy Paxman

The presenter of the BBC news and current affairs programme, Newsnight, *and a writer, radio presenter and chairman of* University Challenge.

'Don't believe anyone who tells you that you'll never be able to do something.'

Boris Johnson MP

The Conservative Member of Parliament for Henley-on-Thames and Editor of The Spectator.

'Do remember, darling, it's not how you're doing, it's what you're doing.'

Grandma

Sir David Jason OBE

*One of the most popular actors on British TV,
whose biggest success was as Del Trotter in*
Only Fools and Horses.

'Look,
learn,
mark and
inwardly digest.'

Philip Pullman

The once teacher and lecturer, now writer of children's books – his most well-known, the award-winning trilogy His Dark Materials.

Philip Pullman

'Yo no soy aquel yo soy,
yo soy aquel yo sera.'
'I am not what I am – I am what I shall be.'

From a Chilean political song

Brendan Foster MBE

The former world-class long-distance runner, Olympic medallist and 3000m world record-holder, and television athletics commentator. He has a leading role in the organization of the Great North Run.

'It is not the critic who counts, not the man who points out how the strong man stumbled, or where the doer of deeds could have done better. The credit belongs to the man who is actually in the arena; whose face is marred by dust and sweat and blood; who strives valiantly; who errs and comes short again and again; who knows the great enthusiasms, the great devotions and spends himself in a worthy cause; who at the best knows in the end the triumph of high achievement, and who, at worst, if he fails, at least fails while daring greatly; so that his place shall never be with those cold and timid souls who know neither victory nor defeat.'

Theodore Roosevelt

Sir Patrick Moore CBE

The astronomer and author of over 70 books on astronomy, and well-known and loved presenter on British television of the long-running series The Sky at Night. *He served as a navigator in RAF Bomber Command during World War II. He was involved in the lunar mapping used by the NASA Apollo space missions.*

'War among us is a survival from savage times, and affects now chiefly the boyish and unthinking element of the nation. It is something a people outgrow. The wisest among us realise that there are better ways of practising heroism.'

Percival Lowell, *Mars and Its Canals*, 1906

Sir Derek Jacobi CBE

One of Britain's best-known actors on TV, stage and big screen, playing Emperor Claudius in the BBC drama I, Claudius *and appearing in many Shakespeare adaptations.*

'There's a special providence in the fall of a sparrow; if it be now, 'tis not to come, if it be not to come it will be now, if it be not now, yet it will come. The readiness is all.'

Shakespeare's Hamlet

John McCririck

The racing expert and commentator often seen on racecourses in a deerstalker and cape. He is an award-winning journalist.

'Never forget work comes first.'

Dame Glenda Jackson MP

*The actress and Labour Member of Parliament for
Hampstead and Highgate.*

'Only Connect.'

E.M. Forster

Lord Patrick Lichfield

The 5th Earl of Lichfield and one of the UK's best-known photographers.

'Rules for life

Rule 1
Life is not fair, get used to it.

Rule 2
The world will not care about your self-esteem. The world will expect you to accomplish something BEFORE you feel good about yourself.

Rule 3
You will NOT make £40,000 a year right out of school. You will not be a Chief Executive with car phone until you earn both.

Rule 4
If you think your teacher is tough, wait till you get a boss.

Rule 5
Flipping burgers is not beneath your dignity.

Rule 6
If you mess up; it is not your parents' fault, so do not whine about your mistakes; learn by them.

Rule 7
Before you were born, your parents were not as boring as they are now. They became that way from paying your bills, cleaning your clothes and listening to you talk about how cool you are. So before you save the rain forest from the parasites of your parents' generation, try delousing the wardrobe in your own room.

Rule 8
Your school may have done away with winners and losers, but life has not. Some schools have abolished failing grades and they will give you as many times as you want to get the right answer. This does not bear the slightest resemblance to ANYTHING in real life.

Rule 9
Life is not divided into terms. You do not get summers off, and very few employers are interested in helping you find yourself. Do that in your own time.

Rule 10
Television is NOT real life. In real life people actually have to leave the coffee shop to go to jobs.

Rule 11
Be nice to nerds. The chances are you will end up working for one.'

Aisling McCann

Aisling became Newcomer Primary World Line Dancing Champion in America in 2003, aged 9, just after her beloved sister Aine died, aged 8, from a virus called Myocarditis that had attacked her heart.

'Here is something my mum always says to me:

"If it's for you it will not pass you."

This helps me when I'm in a tough situation, or don't always get the result I want. When I keep this saying in my mind I know whatever the end result is it is meant to be.'

After Aine – her best buddy in the whole world – died suddenly at Christmas 2002, Aisling felt a big hole in her life and has found that her dancing has kept her going as she gets so lonely when she thinks about her. She misses Aine terribly. The hospital looking after Aine had mistakenly been treating her for diabetes.

Colin Jackson CBE

The Olympic athlete, hurdler and 110m runner.

**'If at first you
don't succeed,
pick yourself up
and try again.'**

Susannah York

Susannah York

'In the midst of winter I finally learned there was in me an invincible summer.'

Albert Camus

Dave Pelzer

Identified as one of the most severely abused children in California, Dave went on to write of his experiences in A Child Called 'It', The Lost Boy *and* A Man Named Dave.

'Above all, if you believe in yourself and your just cause, you can change the course of the world!'

Jo Durie

The former professional tennis player who won
seven national titles.

'Life does not have a destination:
only a journey.'

Sheila Hancock OBE

The British actress and director, who first became famous on TV in The Rag Trade. *A versatile actress who has appeared in radio panel games, musicals such as* Annie, *stage and TV dramas, comedies, and Shakespeare with the Royal Shakespeare Company.*

'There's only one corner of the universe you can be certain of improving and that's your own self.'

Aldous Huxley

Jonathan Edwards CBE

The former British triple jumper, Olympic gold medallist and world record holder. He retired in 2003 as Great Britain's most medalled athlete, and is currently a television presenter and sports commentator.

'Life breaks us all . . . but some of us are made stronger at the broken places.'

Ernest Hemingway

Ken Dodd OBE

The entertainer, comedian, singer and actor.

'All the world's a stage, And all the men and women merely players.'

Shakespeare's Jaques in *As You Like It*

Steve Cram MBE

The athlete, with three gold medals at the Commonwealth Games, the setter of three world records, and BBC TV Sports Personality of the Year. He is a television commentator and presenter, President of the National Boys and Girls' Club, and London Marathon runner in aid of charity.

'If a man is called to be a streetsweeper, he should sweep streets as Michelangelo painted, or Beethoven composed music, or Shakespeare wrote poetry. He should sweep streets so well that all the hosts of heaven and earth will pause to say, here lived a great streetsweeper who did his job well.'

Martin Luther King Jnr

The Rt Hon Michael Howard QC MP

The Leader of the Opposition and Member of Parliament for Folkestone and Hythe.

'God, grant me the serenity to accept the things I cannot change, courage to change the things I can, and wisdom to know the difference.'

Reinhold Niebuhr

Professor Andrew Motion

The writer, Professor of Poetry, and Poet Laureate since 1999.

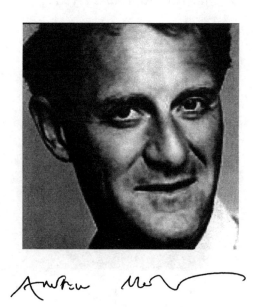

'The imagination may be compared to Adam's dream – he awoke and found it true.'

From a letter by John Keats

Paul Daniels

The world-famous magician and entertainer.

'In life there are really only two things to worry about. Those are the things that you can do something about, and those that you can't.

Now let's think about that; if you can't do anything about it, then there is no point in worrying because it will have no affect (except on yourself) and it will be of no use whatsoever. Get on with your life and have fun without hurting anyone else.

If you *can* do something about it, stop putting it off. *Do it now* and get the situation sorted.

Dawdling will only increase stress and worry for yourself and all those who love you. Then, when you have dealt with it, get on with your life and have fun without hurting anyone else.'

My father, Handel Newton Daniels

James Cracknell MBE

The World and Olympic Champion rower and member of the triumphant coxless four crew at the Sydney Olympics, and regular sports columnist for The Daily Telegraph *since 1998*

'If I had six hours to chop down a tree, I'd spend the first four sharpening the axe.'

Abraham Lincoln

Konnie Huq

The presenter of BBC Blue Peter *and* UK Top 40.

'Yesterday is history.
Tomorrow is a mystery.
Today is a gift – that is why
we call it the present!'

Ivan Henderson

The Member of Parliament for Harwich 1997–2005.
Before becoming an MP, he worked as a docker in
Harwich for three years to 1994.

'Slow Dance

Have you ever watched kids on a merry-go-round?
Or listened to the rain slapping on the ground?
Ever followed a butterfly's erratic flight?
Or gazed at the sun into the fading night?
You'd better slow down
Don't dance so fast
Time is short
The music won't last

Do you run through each day on the fly?
When you ask "How are you?" Do you hear the reply?
When the day is done, do you lie in your bed
With the next hundred chores running through your
     head?
You'd better slow down
Don't dance so fast
Time is short
The music won't last

Ever told your child, we'll do it tomorrow?
And in your haste, not see his sorrow?
Ever lost touch, let a good friendship die?
'Cause you never had time to call and say "hi"
You'd better slow down
Don't dance so fast
Time is short
The music won't last

When you run so fast to get somewhere
You miss half the fun of getting there
When you worry and hurry through your day
It's like an unopened gift, thrown away.
Life is not a race
Do take it slower
Hear the music
Before the song is over.'

This poem was discovered on a windowsill at Great
Ormond Street Hospital, London.

Michael Morpurgo MBE

*The writer of 100 books, and Children's Laureate
2003–05. His books have been adapted for cinema,
television and theatre, and he has won numerous awards.
He and his wife were awarded the MBE for their charitable
work with Farms for City Children.*

**'Live every day to the full, not as if it is
your last, but as if it is your first.'**

John McEnroe

The number one tennis player in the world four times between 1981 and 1984. After 'retiring', John became the Davis Cup team coach and a television tennis commentator.

'It is far better to go out, try your best at something and fail, than it is to have not tried at all.'

Jean Ure

The top-selling children's author.

'Not until we extend the circle or our
compassion to all living things shall we
ourselves know peace.'

Albert Schweitzer

Jasper Carrott

The English comedian and sit-com actor.

'Luck is when preparation meets opportunity.'

Mark Cox MBE

The tennis player who in 1968 became the first amateur to beat a professional and herald the beginning of the Open era. He is the only post-war player to be in the British Davis Cup teams that reached both the Semi Final and Final of the Davis Cup. He was team member during 1967–79, and was six times ranked the number one British tennis player. He is a patron of CRY.

'In every cloud there is a silver lining.'

Anna Ford

*The British broadcasting journalist, and the BBC
One O'Clock News presenter.*

Anna Ford.

'To be what we are, and to become
what we are capable of becoming, is the
only end in life.'

Robert Louis Stevenson

Dr Liam Fox MP

The Conservative Member of Parliament for Woodspring since 1992 and Shadow Foreign Secretary since May 2005. He was Co-Chairman of the Conservative Party in 2003–05.

'So many worlds, so much to do,
So little done, such things to be.'

From *In Memoriam* by Alfred, Lord Tennyson

Geraldine McCaughrean

The award-winning author who has been writing children's books for over 20 years; she has written more than 120 books.

'Nulla dies sine linea.'
'Not a day without a line.'

Latin proverb

Richard Briers CBE

The well-known and loved English actor who became a household name in The Good Life, *he has been recognized for his services to drama in his career in TV, film and theatre. His work includes classical and leading Shakespearean roles.*

'There's a special providence in the fall of a sparrow; if it be now, 'tis not to come, if it be not to come, it will be now, if it be not now, yet it will come. The readiness is all.'

Shakespeare's
Hamlet

Noel Edmonds

The television and radio presenter, media personality and businessman.

'The only place where success comes before work is in the dictionary!'

Vince Lombardi

Sir Trevor Brooking CBE

The football broadcaster and former midfielder for West Ham and England (capped 47 times), and the Chairman of Sport England.

'If

If you can keep your head when all about you
Are losing theirs and blaming it on you,
If you can trust yourself when all men doubt you
But make allowance for their doubting too,
If you can wait and not be tired by waiting,
Or being lied about, don't deal in lies,
Or being hated, don't give way to hating,
And yet don't look too good, nor talk too wise:

If you can dream – and not make dreams your master,
If you can think – and not make thoughts your aim;
If you can meet with Triumph and Disaster
And treat those two impostors just the same;
If you can bear to hear the truth you've spoken
Twisted by knaves to make a trap for fools,
Or watch the things you gave your life to, broken,
And stoop and build 'em up with worn-out tools:

If you can make one heap of all your winnings
And risk it all on one turn of pitch-and-toss,
And lose, and start again at your beginnings
And never breathe a word about your loss;
If you can force your heart and nerve and sinew
To serve your turn long after they are gone,
And so hold on when there is nothing in you
Except the Will which says to them: "Hold on!"

If you can talk with crowds and keep your virtue,
Or walk with kings – nor lose the common touch,
If neither foes nor loving friends can hurt you;
If all men count with you, but none too much,
If you can fill the unforgiving minute
With sixty seconds' worth of distance run,
Yours is the Earth and everything that's in it,
And – which is more – you'll be a Man, my son!'

Rudyard Kipling

Lord Sebastian Coe MBE

The British runner, with two Olympic gold medals and twelve broken world records. Upon retirement he was elected to Parliament as a Conservative MP 1992–97. He was Chairman of the successful London bid for the 2012 Olympics, a writer, broadcaster and public speaker.

'Ask not what your country can do for you – ask what you can do for your country.'

J.F. Kennedy,
Inaugural Address,
20 January 1961

Geoff Sewell

The classically trained singer and founding member of
Amici Forever, The Opera Band.

'Life is a daring adventure or nothing!'

Helen Keller

Anne Fine

The writer, Children's Laureate 2001–03, Carnegie Medal winner, Whitbread Children's Book of the Year Award and Smarties Prize winner. She is the author of Madame Doubtfire, *now a major film.*

'Wisdom is the principal thing.
Therefore get wisdom. But with all thy
getting, get understanding.'

Proverbs 4.7

Geoffrey Boycott

The cricket commentator and former England and Yorkshire batsman.

'Speak the truth and fear no man.'

Lucy Briers

The actress on television, radio and theatre, and the daughter of Richard Briers CBE.

'You can't remake the world
Without remaking yourself.
Each new era begins within.
it is an inward event,

With unsuspected possibilities
For inner liberation.
We could use it to turn on
Our inward lights.
We could use it to use even the dark
And negative things positively.
We could use the new era
To clean our eyes,
To see the world differently,
To see ourselves more clearly.
Only free people can make a free world.
Infect the world with your light.
help fulfil the golden prophecies.
Press forward the human genius.
Our future is greater than our past.'

From 'The Mental Flight' by Ben Okri

Frances Edmonds

*The author, broadcaster and public speaker, and the wife
of international cricketer Phil Edmonds.*

Frances Edmonds

'You are not a failure if you don't succeed; you're a success because you try.'

The Rt Hon
Charles Clarke MP

*The Home Secretary since December 2004, and
Member of Parliament for Norwich South (Labour).*

'Look for the hero inside of you.'

Nick Butterworth

One of the most popular and talented authors and illustrator of children's books, including his most famous creation, Percy the Park Keeper *stories.*

'"Rabbit's clever," said Pooh thoughtfully. "Yes," said Piglet, "Rabbit's clever." "And he has Brain." "Yes," said Piglet, "Rabbit has Brain." There was a long silence. "I suppose," said Pooh, "that's why he never understands anything." "Supposing a tree fell down, Pooh, when we were underneath it?" "Supposing it didn't," said Pooh after careful thought. Piglet was comforted by this.'

From *The House At Pooh Corner* © A. A. Milne. Copyright under the Berne Convention. Published by Egmont Books Limited, London and used with permission.

Honor Blackman

The actress particularly remembered as Pussy Galore in Goldfinger *and Cathy Gale in* The Avengers *in the 1960s.*

'Hitch your
wagon to a star.'

Ralph Waldo Emerson

'This above all,
to thine own self
be true.'

Shakespeare's Polonius
in *Hamlet*

Ian Botham OBE

*The legendary England cricketer and former captain.
A broadcaster, commentator and writer famous for his
charitable endeavours, he is President of CRY.*

'Ride the torpedo to the end of the tube.'

Jeremy Clarkson

*The journalist, broadcaster, and presenter of BBC's
Top Gear, Jeremy recently discovered his ancestry in the
BBC 2 series* Who Do You Think You Are?

'Tired of lying in the sunshine
Staying home to watch the rain
And you are young and life is long
And there is time to kill today
And then one day you find
Ten years have got behind you
No one told you when to run
You missed the starting gun.'

Pink Floyd, 'Time'

Consent to include lyrics from 'Time' by Pink Floyd Management
Ltd, 26 January 2005.

The Rt Hon
David Blunkett MP

The Member of Parliament for Sheffield since 1987
(Labour) and Home Secretary 2001–04.

'Success in life is having the confidence to never take no for an answer, when you know in your heart that the answer shouldn't be no! For patience, persistence and tenacity, should blend nicely with endeavour, to make success a reality.'

Chris Moon MBE

The former army officer who lost his lower right leg and arm when helping to clear landmines in Mozambique. He is a public speaker whose enthusiasm for life is inspirational.

'Success is about getting up one more time than you fall over – even if you don't have a leg to stand on. The great thing is to keep on keeping on.'

Val Biro

Born and trained as an artist in Hungary, he is the illustrator and writer of the popular children's series based on the real Gumdrop, his own 1926 Austin 12/4 Heavy car.

self-portrait in GUMDROP

'There are more things in heaven and
earth, Horatio,
Than are dreamt of in your philosophy.'

Shakespeare's Hamlet

Jonny Wilkinson OBE

*The English rugby union player who made worldwide
headlines in 2003 when he kicked the winning drop goal in
the last minute of the Rugby World Cup against Australia.
He was voted BBC Sports Personality of the Year, and
named Captain of the England team in October 2004.*

'I can't always succeed but I can always deserve to.'

Daniel O'Donnell MBE

The popular Irish singer who received the MBE for his services to the music industry.

'Yesterday is history.
Tomorrow is a mystery.
Today is a gift – that is
why we call it the present!'

Russ Abbot

The British comedian voted 'Funniest Man on TV', and a
regular in many pantomimes and summer shows including
A Midsummer Night's Dream *as Bottom.*

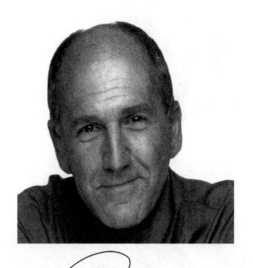

'Never put off today what
you can do tomorrow,
because if you like it today
you can do it again tomorrow!'

Roger Black MBE

The former athlete – 400m double Commonwealth and European Gold Medallist in 1986, double European Gold Medallist again in 1990, and Olympic Silver Medal in 1996. He is currently a television presenter and public speaker.

'The essence lies not in the victory but in the struggle.'

Olympic motto

Martin Bell OBE

The former foreign affairs correspondent, Independent Member of Parliament 1997–2001, and UNICEF Ambassador for Humanitarian Emergencies.

'He has achieved success who has lived well, laughed often and loved much:
Who has gained the respect of intelligent men and the love of children:
Who has filled his mind, accomplished many tasks:
Who leaves the world better than he found it:
Who never lacked appreciation of earth's beauty or failed to express it:
Who looked for the best in others and gave the best he had:
His life was an inspiration
His memory is a benediction.'

Robert Louis Stevenson (attributed)

Sir Jonathan Sacks

The Chief Rabbi of the United Hebrew Congregations of the Commonwealth.

'Each time a man stands up for an ideal, or acts to improve the lot of others, or strikes out against injustice, he sends forth a tiny ripple of hope, and crossing each other from a million different centres of energy and daring, those ripples build a current that can sweep down the mightiest walls of oppression and resistance.'

Robert F. Kennedy

Jeremy Vine

The former reporter on the Today *programme, who then moved to Westminster as a political correspondent. He presented* Newsnight *and now has his own show on BBC Radio 2.*

'There's more to life than books, but not much more.'

Morrissey

Sir Ranulph Fiennes OBE

The explorer who has led over 20 expeditions to remote parts of the world. In 2003 he completed seven marathons in seven days, in seven different countries. He was awarded the OBE for human endeavour and charitable services.

'Whatever you can do, or dream you can . . . begin it.'

Goethe

Pam Ayres MBE

The British writer of humorous poetry, broadcaster and entertainer who was awarded the MBE for services to literature and entertainment in June 2004.

'Oh, to be only half as wonderful as my children <u>once</u> thought I was and only half as stupid as they think I am now.'

Sir James Galway OBE

The world-leading flutist from Belfast, often called 'the man with the golden flute'; most recently he recorded the soundtracks of the Lord of the Rings *film trilogy.*

'Failing to prepare is like preparing to fail.'

Benjamin Franklin

Dora Bryan OBE

One of Britain's favourite character actors, playing mainly eccentric roles, she has portrayed many a Cockney and Northerner in her long film career.

'God, grant me the serenity to accept the things I cannot change, courage to change the things I can, and wisdom to know the difference.'

Reinhold Niebuhr

Dickie Bird MBE

The umpire of first-class and Test cricket, holding the world record for umpiring 160 international matches. He played cricket for Yorkshire and Leicestershire, 1956–66, was Yorkshire Man of the Year 1996, and is the author of best-selling books.

'The good Lord gave everyone a gift. You must use that gift to the very best of your ability. Work very hard at that gift and you will then succeed in life, and get to the top of whatever profession you choose, and thank the Lord Jesus for this.'

Dickie Bird MBE

The Very Revd
Dr John Moses OBE

The Dean of St Paul's Cathedral since 1996.

'I am part of all that I have met;
Yet all experience is an arch
wherethrough
Gleams that untravelled world,
whose margin fades
For ever and for ever when I move.
How dull it is to pause, to make
and end,
To rust unburnished, not to shine
in use!
As though to breathe were life ...

Though much is taken, much
abides; and though
We are not now that strength
which in old days
Moved earth and heaven; that
which we are, we are;
One equal temper of heroic hearts,
Made weak by time and fate, but strong in will
To strive, to seek, to find, and not to yield.'

Extract from 'Ulysses' by Alfred, Lord Tennyson

As Tennyson tells the story in his poem, Ulysses is now an old man but is
reluctant to let go of life, and I think the words say something about the spirit of
adventure and the resolution that seem to me to be so important.

Liz Barker

The BBC Blue Peter *presenter from* 2000.

'To love oneself is the beginning of a life-long romance.'

Oscar Wilde

The Rt Hon Tony Benn

*The former Labour MP and Cabinet Minister, and
long-time peace campaigner and author.*

'Do not stand at my grave
  and weep
I am not there, I do not sleep.
I am a thousand winds that
  blow.
I am the diamond glint on
  snow.
I am sunlight on ripened
  grain,
I am the gentle autumn rain.
When you awaken in the
  morning's hush
I am the swift uplifting rush
Of quiet birds in circled
  flight.
I am the soft stars that shine
  at night.
Do not stand at my grave
  and cry
I am not there, I did not die.'

Mary Frye

Major General Patrick Cordingley DSO

The former Commander of the Desert Rats, the 7th Armoured Brigade, during the first Gulf War, awarded the Distinguished Service Order for his bravery and leadership. He is a writer and public speaker.

'You do not need to be a brilliant speaker to be effective. Two things are necessary: first to know what you are talking about, and second to believe it yourself.'

Bruce Oldfield OBE

The world-leading fashion designer who has designed outfits for many famous celebrities and members of the British and European aristocracy; he is a committed supporter of Barnado's children's charity.

'I noticed that whenever I moved things out of the reach of my border terrier puppy, the more determined he would be to stretch his little legs that extra inch to get what he wanted. It occurred to me that that's what life's all about, that little extra effort for well-earned rewards.'

Sir Alan Ayckbourn CBE

The English playwright and director, knighted for his services to theatre. He has written more then 60 plays and won numerous awards. His plays have been translated into 35 languages and performed on stage and television throughout the world. Some feature on school curricula for study and examination.

'You don't get to choose how you're going to die, or when. You can only decide how you're going to live. Now.'

Joan Baez

Sir Michael Caine CBE

One of Britain's most outstanding and successful actors.

'Success usually comes to those who are too busy to be looking for it.'

Henry David Thoreau

Jeremy Bates

*The professional tennis player and British Davis Cup
Captain, London Marathon runner for charity,
and Patron of CRY.*

'I'm a great believer in luck and I find
the harder I work, the more I have of it.'

Thomas Jefferson, third President of the USA

Anthea Turner

The television presenter who became famous as a
BBC Blue Peter *presenter.*

Anthea Turner

'Aim to be the best and the rest will follow.'

Jonathan Pugh

Cartoonist for The Times.

Jonathan Pugh

'I am always doing things I can't do, that's how I get to do them.'

Picasso

Stirling Moss

A pioneer in British Formula One racing, he has participated in around 525 races, winning 16 Formula One Grand Prix

'Movement is tranquillity.'

Rob Andrew

The former England rugby player, who was appointed Director of Rugby at Newcastle Falcons in 1995. He is England's most capped fly-half, with 70 caps and a score total of 396 points.

'Always focus on trying to be a little bit better every day. Sometimes this is difficult even for the most enthusiastic people, but they always find a way. This is everyone's challenge, every day.'

Cherie Blair

The prime minister's wife, who also practices under her maiden name, Cherie Booth, as a Queen's Counsel for a London law firm.

'What lies behind us and what lies before us are tiny matters compared to what lies within us.'

Ralph Waldo Emerson

Dear Julie,

The Holy Father has received your letter and he has asked me to thank you. He appreciates the concerns which prompted you to write to him.

His Holiness will remember you and your work in his prayers. He encourages you in all that you are doing to support the families of young people who die unexpectedly. Bringing comfort to those who mourn is a truly Christ-like act of charity.

Upon you and your family he invokes God's blessings of joy and peace.

From the Vatican, 13 November 2004

A–Z Index

Index by Subject